Get **more** out of libraries

Please return or renew this item by the last date shown.
You can renew online at www.hants.gov.uk/library
Or by phoning 0845 603 5631

nasen

nasen
NASEN House, 4/5 Amber Business Village, Amber Close,
Amington, Tamworth, Staffordshire B77 4RP

Rising Stars UK Ltd.
22 Grafton Street, London W1S 4EX
www.risingstars-uk.com

Every effort has been made to trace copyright holders and
obtain their permission for use of copyright material. The
publisher will gladly receive information enabling them to
rectify any error or omission in subsequent editions.
All facts are correct at time of going to press.

First published 2007

Cover design: Button plc
Cover image: Alamy
Text design and typesetting: Andy Wilson
Publisher: Gill Budgell
Project management and editorial: Lesley Densham
Editing: Clare Robertson
Editorial consultants: Cliff Moon, Lorraine Petersen and
Frances Ridley
Technical adviser: Mandy Holloway (NHM)
Illustrations: Chris King: pages 22–23, 30–31, 36–39
Oxford Illustrators and Designers: pages 13, 14, 27
Photos: Alamy: pages 4–5, 7, 10, 14–15, 19, 20, 25, 32, 35,
40, 41, 43
Corbis: pages 6, 9, 19, 24–25, 28, 29, 35, 43
Getty Images: pages 8, 11, 12, 13, 15, 16–17, 18, 21, 26–27,
33, 41, 42, 43,
Kobal: page 34
TopFoto: pages 6–7

British Library Cataloguing in Publication Data.
A CIP record for this book is available from the
British Library.

ISBN: 978-1-84680-189-1

Printed by Craft Print International Limited, Singapore

Contents

The power of nature 4

Famous natural disasters 6

Meet the experts 8

Emergency teams 10

Earthquakes 12

Tsunamis 14

Case study: emergency aid 16

Volcanoes 18

Tornado Trouble – Part one 22

Hurricanes 24

Tornadoes 26

Floods and landslides 28

Tornado Trouble – Part two 30

Drought and forest fires 32

Natural disasters @ the movies 34

Tornado Trouble – Part three 36

Future fears 40

Global warming 42

Quiz 44

Glossary of terms 45

More resources 46

Answers 47

Index 48

The power of nature

Earthquakes and volcanoes shake the earth.

Hurricanes and tsunamis destroy cities and kill thousands.

These natural disasters show us the power of nature.

Disaster fact!

There are almost 400 natural disasters every year.

Famous natural disasters

Some natural disasters go down in history.

Pompeii

In AD 79, Mount Vesuvius erupted. It buried the town of Pompeii under piles of ash.

Everyone living there was killed.

Krakatoa

The volcano Krakatoa exploded in 1883. It destroyed an island.

The blast had the force of a million atomic bombs.

It sent out an ash cloud 80 kilometres high and a tsunami with 36-metre high waves.

San Francisco

In 1906, a massive earthquake rocked San Francisco.

The San Andreas fault ripped open for over 430 kilometres.

The quake sparked fires that burned for three days.

Thousands died or were made homeless.

Meet the experts

Scientists try to predict natural disasters.
They use **sensors**, **radars** and **satellites**
to collect data.

Scientists study
the patterns of
seismic waves and
compare them to
those recorded on
previous occasions.

Then the scientists feed the data
into a computer.

This is a computer model of a tsunami. It helps scientists to predict whether the tsunami will reach the land.

Animals may be experts too. Some scientists think animals can sense natural disasters before they happen. But there is no proof.

Elephants screamed and ran for higher ground before the tsunami in Indonesia in 2004.

Emergency teams

Emergency teams are trained to deal with natural disasters. They travel into disaster areas to save lives.

Search and rescue teams

Search and rescue teams search for people trapped after earthquakes and other disasters.

They work with dogs and robots. They use **infrared cameras** to help them find people.

Aid agencies

Aid agencies set up tents and emergency hospitals to treat the injured.

They send in food, water, clothes and blankets.
They help to reunite families.

The Army

Armies bring in emergency aid by road and air.

They help to rescue survivors.

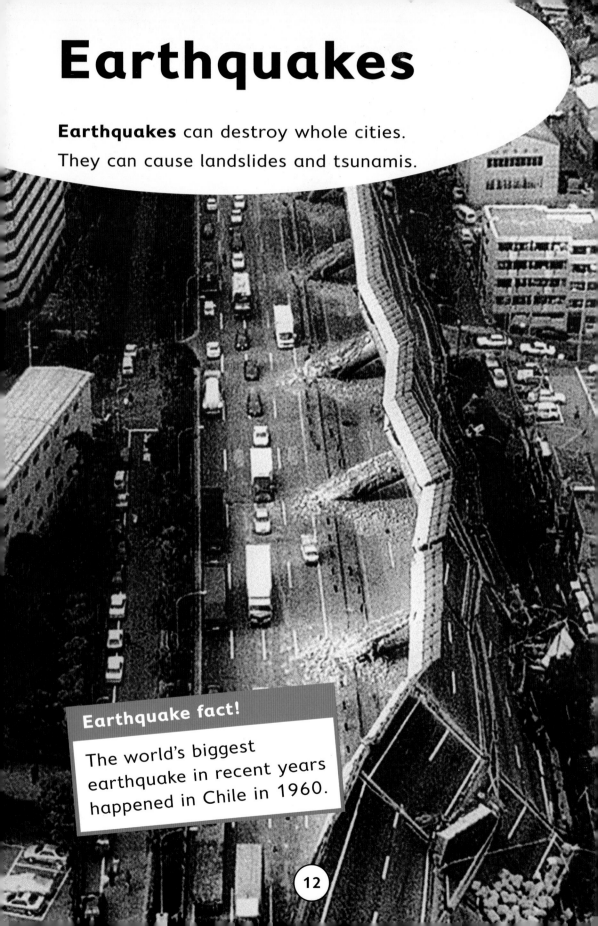

Earthquakes

Earthquakes can destroy whole cities.
They can cause landslides and tsunamis.

Earthquake fact!

The world's biggest earthquake in recent years happened in Chile in 1960.

How do they happen?

Earth's crust is made up of plates, or layers of rock. The plates meet at **fault lines**.

Sometimes the plates clash together and cause an earthquake.

The place where this happens is called the epicentre.

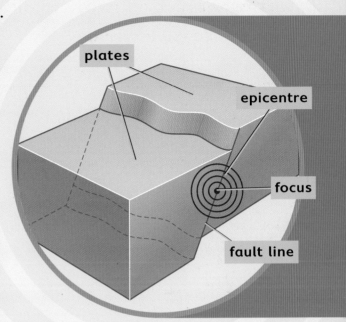

plates

epicentre

focus

fault line

Scientists measure earthquakes on a **seismometer**.

Tsunamis

A tsunami is a giant wave.

Tsunami waves can be 200 kilometres long. They can travel hundreds of kilometres and reach speeds of up to 800 kph.

Tsunami fact!

Tsunami waves get taller as they reach coastal waters.

How do they happen?

An earthquake lifts part of the seabed. This pushes up vast amounts of water.

Huge waves moved out from the epicentre.

2004 Tsunami

On December the 26th 2004, a huge earthquake rocked the Indian ocean. It caused a tsunami that killed thousands of people.

The Indonesian coastline

Before the tsunami

After the tsunami

Case study: emergency aid

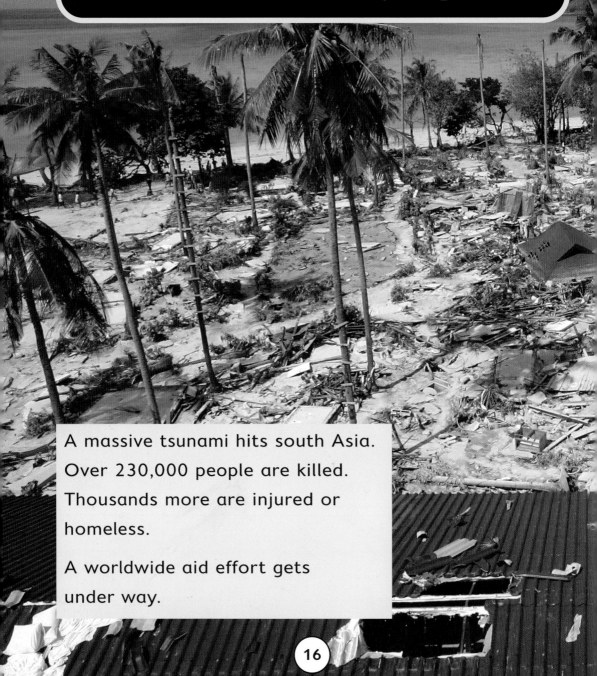

00.58.51 GMT. Boxing Day 2004

A massive tsunami hits south Asia. Over 230,000 people are killed. Thousands more are injured or homeless.

A worldwide aid effort gets under way.

Food, water, shelter, blankets and medicine are sent in ships and planes.

Trucks and helicopters take the aid to the people who need it.

A single air drop can deliver 18 tonnes of aid.

Volcanoes

Our planet has a core of fire deep under the earth's crust. Sometimes hot rock and gas have to escape. They burst out through volcanoes.

Volcanoes can be dramatic and deadly.

They can bury towns under ash and **lava**.

They can set off tsunamis and black out the sun.

Mount St Helens in Washington, United States, erupted in 1980. It killed 58 people and caused damage costing $1 billion.

The force of the blast reached over 1000 kph. People heard the blast in Canada!

Volcano fact!

Undersea volcanoes sometimes erupt to make new islands.

The deadliest volcanoes of all are under the earth. They are called **supervolcanoes**.

One of the biggest supervolcanoes is under Yellowstone National Park in the United States. It erupts about every 600,000 years.

The last eruption was 640,000 years ago!

Scientists use instruments to 'listen' to active volcanoes.

They take temperature data from **satellites**.

They use **sensors** to 'sniff' changes in volcano gases from 20 kilometres away.

Studying volcanoes can still be a deadly job. In 1993, six scientists were killed in Colombia. They were studying the crater of an active volcano when it suddenly erupted.

Tornado Trouble
(Part one)

"Hurry up, Carl!"

Mr Thomson sounded a bit cross now.

Carl was making a volcano and the rest of the class had finished theirs. But Carl wanted his to be a supervolcano. He had built the model and painted it. Now he just had to put the mix in. What had Mr Thomson said? Mix up the soap and baking soda … pour that in. Now, add the vinegar and stand well back …

BOOM!

Carl's volcano had exploded all over
the classroom.

There were bits of froth on the whiteboard.
There was even a bit on Mr Thomson's tie.
The whole class was laughing … except for
Mr Thomson. He looked like he would be
the next to explode.

Continued on page 30

Hurricanes

Hurricanes are powerful storms.
They are also called **typhoons** or **cyclones**.

On land, they can destroy trees, cars and
houses. They can even wipe out whole cities.

Hurricane facts!

Hurricanes always circle
around an eye.

Hurricanes are given names
in the order of the alphabet.

Scientists can predict the path and strength of a hurricane. They use computers to help them.

Hurricane hunters fly aircraft into hurricanes to get data.

Tornadoes

A tornado is a tunnel of fast-moving wind. **Tornadoes** are also called **twisters**. They can suck up cows and cars and make buildings explode.

How do they happen?

1. Warm air and cold air come together.

2. Storm clouds form and start to circle.

3. The warm air gets sucked upwards.

4. It makes a funnel of wind that spins faster and faster.

Tornado fact!

Tornadoes are measured on the Fujita scale from F0 to F5. F5s can reach speeds of over 320 kph and damage concrete buildings.

The United States gets more tornadoes than any other country.

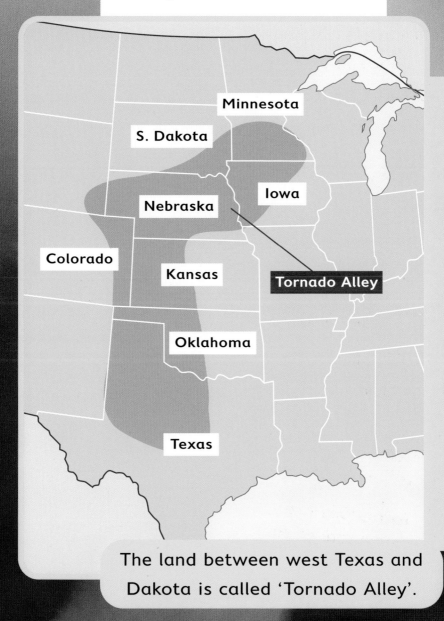

Minnesota

S. Dakota

Iowa

Nebraska

Colorado

Kansas

Tornado Alley

Oklahoma

Texas

The land between west Texas and Dakota is called 'Tornado Alley'.

Floods and landslides

Floods

Floods can be caused by:

- ◎ heavy rain
- ◎ melting snow

- ◎ rivers bursting their banks
- ◎ storm surges on the coast.

Some floods happen without warning.
They are called 'flash-floods'.

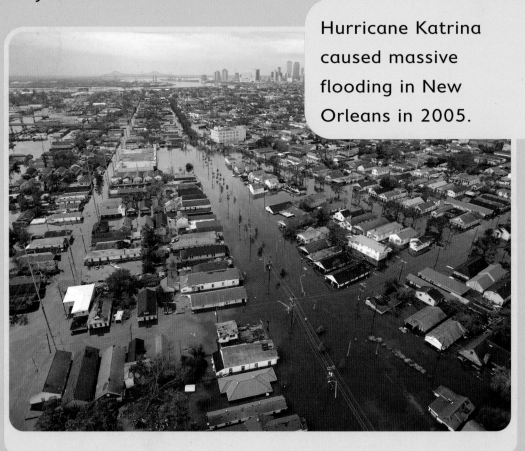

Hurricane Katrina caused massive flooding in New Orleans in 2005.

Landslides

Landslides can bury villages and kill thousands of people.

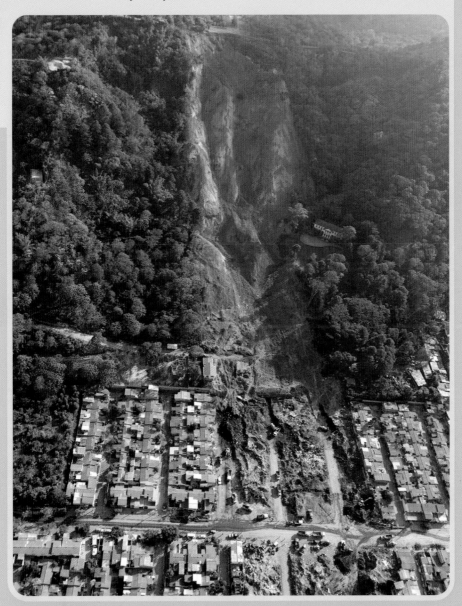

A landslide can be caused by rain.

The rain breaks up mud on the mountain side.

Then the mud slides down the mountain.

Tornado Trouble
(Part two)

Mr Thomson had not forgotten the volcano episode. He had his eye on Carl.

"Are you listening, Carl?"

"Mm ... yes, Mr Thomson."

Carl was looking out of the window. Something odd was happening out there.

The sky had gone dark. Hail was rattling against the windows. The wind was getting up. A paper bag swirled round the playground.

"So what is the difference between a hurricane and a typhoon?"

"A tornado … I think it's a tornado," Carl muttered.

"Not a tornado!" Mr Thomson thundered. "We're doing tornadoes next week!"

But Carl wasn't listening. He was watching the huge black cloud. It was getting nearer and nearer.

Continued on page 36

Drought and forest fires

Drought

A drought happens when there is no rain for a long time.

The earth cracks, crops don't grow and animals and people die.

Drought can last for months or even years.

Forest fires

Forests get very dry during
a drought. Forest fires start
easily and spread quickly.

Natural disasters @ the movies

Movie heroes often fight natural disasters.

They save the world from destruction.
But could it really happen?

The Core (2003)

Natural disaster The earth has stopped spinning.
This sets off huge electrical storms.

What do they do? Use a massive explosion to
set it spinning again.

Could it happen? Scientists don't think the Earth
will ever stop spinning.

Armageddon (1995)

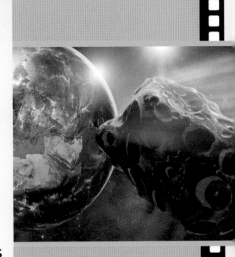

Natural disaster An asteroid the size of Texas is about to collide with Earth.

What do they do? Drill a hole in the asteroid. Then blast it apart with explosives.

Could it happen? Yes, but asteroids this big only come around every 50 to 100 million years!

The Day After Tomorrow (2004)

Natural disaster The polar ice caps have melted. This causes massive storms and a new ice age.

What do they do? Go into hiding until the storms blow over.

Could it happen? Climate change is happening – but over years, not days, as in the movie.

Tornado Trouble
(Part three)

"Mr Thomson! It's a tornado … and it's coming towards us!"

Carl jumped up, pointing out of the window.

"Oh yes, very funny," Mr Thomson said. "The only tornado in this classroom is …"

CRASH!

Carl looked outside.

The sky was completely black. The great
black cloud was swirling like a funnel.
It was sucking up everything in its path.

A rubbish bin flew past the window.
Bricks and tiles fell out of the sky.
Car alarms screamed.

"Everybody down!" Mr Thomson shouted.
"Get under the desks!"

Continued on the next page

The school shook. The windows smashed.
Bits of glass went flying.

It lasted less than a minute. Then the sky
got brighter and the noise stopped.

Everyone stood up. They looked out through
the jagged windows.

The fence had been flattened. A car had
been lifted up and dropped by the gates.
The wall of the science block had been
ripped off. You could see the benches inside.

"Everybody all right?" Mr Thomson looked shaken.

He looked at his watch. "14.54 GMT," he said. "And I think we have just had our very own tornado."

"Looks like we're doing tornadoes this week after all!" whispered Carl.

Future fears

Giant asteroids

Some asteroids are more than a kilometre across.

If one hit the sea, it would cause a huge tsunami.

Supervolcanoes

If a supervolcano erupted, its ash would blot out the sun. Earth's climate would change overnight.

Supervolcanoes could even make us extinct!

Solar flares

A giant **solar flare** could knock out our computers and phones. It could leave planet Earth without power.

Mega-tsunamis

A massive landslide in the Canary Islands could trigger a mega-tsunami.

The giant wave would destroy the east coast of America.

Global warming

Global warming is the biggest natural disaster we face today. It is caused by carbon gases from cars and industry which are warming up the planet.

A 3°C to 6°C rise in the next century could spell disaster.

Polar ice caps and glaciers melt.

Sea levels rise, leaving 200 million people homeless.

Crops fail because of drought.

40% of species become extinct.

What would happen?

Violent storms increase.

43

Quiz

1 What happened to Pompeii in AD 79?

2 What can seismic signals help predict?

3 What causes most tsunamis?

4 What are hurricanes also called?

5 What do hurricanes circle around?

6 What is another name for tornadoes?

7 How are tornadoes measured?

8 What is a supervolcano?

9 Where is one of the biggest supervolcanoes situated?

10 How might a giant solar flare affect life on Earth?

Glossary of terms

asteroid	A rocky piece of debris in space.
cyclone	Another name for a hurricane.
earthquake	When the earth's rocks suddenly crack and release shock waves.
epicentre	The centre of an earthquake.
eye	A calm centre which usually develops at the core of a hurricane.
fault line	The lines that show that there has been movement in the earth's crust.
hurricane	A storm, often tropical, with a powerful wind.
infrared cameras	They reveal warm areas where people are or have been.
lava	Hot, liquid rock that flows out from a volcano.
radar	Instrument that detects objects by sending out energy waves.
satellite	An object that orbits the Earth, collecting data.
seismic waves	Shock waves that travel through the earth and can help us to predict volcanic eruptions.
seismometer	An instrument that measures seismic signals.
sensor	Instrument that picks up changes in humidity, temperature and other data.
solar flare	An explosive release of gases and radiation from the Sun.
storm surge	A sudden increase in size and power of waves at sea, caused by storms.
supervolcano	A large underground volcano.
tornado	A tunnel of very fast-moving wind.
tsunami	A giant wave.
twister	Another name for a tornado.
typhoon	Another name for a hurricane.
volcano	A hole, usually in a mountain, from which hot rock and gases erupt from deep beneath the earth's surface.

More resources

Books

Natural Disasters
Clare Watts
Published by Dorling Kindersley Eyewitness Guides
(ISBN 1405313420)
An in-depth look into all kinds of natural disasters.

Violent Volcanoes and Earth-shattering Earthquakes (Horrible Geography)
Anita Ganeri and Mike Phillips
Published by Scholastic (ISBN 0439982618)
An entertaining look at some of nature's nastiest tricks.

Websites

www.phschool.com/science/planetdiary
An up-to-the-minute diary of natural disasters as they happen around the world.

www.esa.int/esaKIDsen/Earth.html
The site for the European Space Agency, with info on planet Earth and natural disasters as seen from radar and satellites.

DVDs

Eyewitness Interactive: Natural Disasters (2003)
Jill Matthews
Dorling Kindersley (Cat. no. B00004TT5U)

Raging Planet: Angry Earth (2005)
Discovery Channel (Cat. no. B0009X74WU)
Earthquakes, avalanches and volcanoes – and some cutting edge technology for advance warnings.

Answers

1 It was destroyed by the eruption of Mount Vesuvius.

2 Volcanoes and earthquakes

3 Undersea earthquakes

4 Typhoons or cyclones

5 An eye

6 Twisters

7 On the Fujita scale 0F – 5F

8 A giant underground volcano

9 Under Yellowstone Park in the United States

10 It could knock out computers and phones and leave us without power.

Index

aid	11, 16–17	ice caps	35, 42
aid agencies	11	Krakatoa	7
air drop	17	lava	18
Army	11	Mount St Helens	19
ash	6, 7, 18	Mount Vesuvius	6
asteroid	6, 7, 18, 35, 40	movies	34–35
Canada	19	Pompeii	6
Canary Islands	41	radars	8
carbon	42	rain	28, 29
Chile	12	San Andreas Fault	7
climate change	35, 40	San Francisco	7
Colombia	21	satellites	8
core	18	seabed	14
crust	13	search and rescue teams	10
cyclone	24	scientists	8–9, 13, 21, 25, 34
drought	32–33, 43	seismic signals	8
earthquake	4, 7, 8, 12–13, 14	seismometer	13
elephants	9	solar flare	41
emergency teams	10–11	storm surges	28
epicentre	13, 14	supervolcanoes	20–21, 22, 40
extinction	40, 43	tornado	22, 26–27, 31, 36, 39
eye	24	'Tornado Alley'	27
fault lines	13	tsunami	4, 7, 8, 14–15, 16–17, 18, 40
floods	28		
forest fires	33	typhoon	24, 31
Fujita scale	26	volcano	4, 7, 8, 18–21, 22, 23
global warming	42–43	United States	19, 20, 27
hurricane	4, 24–25, 31	Yellowstone National Park	20